MEDICAL DETECTING

DETECTING INJURY

by Joanne Mattern

WWW.FOCUSREADERS.COM

Focus Readers is distributed by North Star Editions:
sales@northstareditions.com | 888-417-0195

Produced for Focus Readers by Red Line Editorial.

Content Consultant: Spencer Smith, MD, Radiologist, Texas College of Osteopathic Medicine

Photographs ©: iStockphoto, cover, 1, 6, 8–9, 10, 16, 20; Shutterstock Images, 4–5, 12–13, 15, 18–19, 23, 26–27, 28; Ashley Calingo/US Marine Corps/PFJ Military Collection/Alamy, 25

Library of Congress Cataloging-in-Publication Data
Names: Mattern, Joanne, 1963- author.
Title: Detecting injury / by Joanne Mattern.
Description: Lake Elmo, MN : Focus Readers, [2024] | Series: Medical detecting | Includes bibliographical references and index. | Audience: Grades 4-6
Identifiers: LCCN 2023002922 (print) | LCCN 2023002923 (ebook) | ISBN 9781637396278 (hardcover) | ISBN 9781637396841 (paperback) | ISBN 9781637397930 (ebook pdf) | ISBN 9781637397411 (hosted ebook)
Subjects: LCSH: Wounds and injuries--Diagnosis--Juvenile literature.
Classification: LCC RC86.5 .M375 2024 (print) | LCC RC86.5 (ebook) | DDC 617.1--dc23/eng/20230214
LC record available at https://lccn.loc.gov/2023002922
LC ebook record available at https://lccn.loc.gov/2023002923

Printed in the United States of America
Mankato, MN
082023

ABOUT THE AUTHOR

Joanne Mattern has written hundreds of books for children. Her favorite subjects include science, biography, history, and sports. She lives in New York state with her family and several pets.

TABLE OF CONTENTS

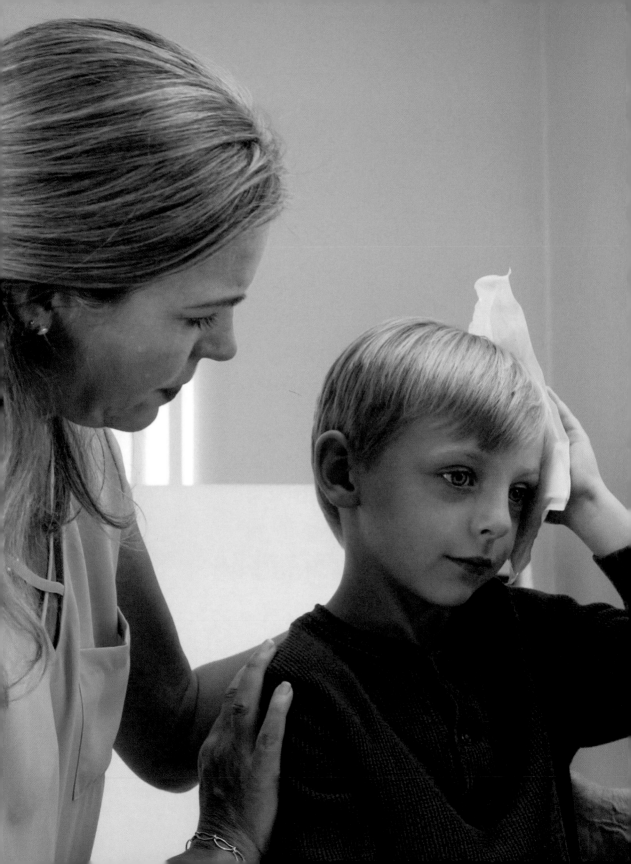

CHAPTER 1

EMERGENCY!

A doctor steps into the emergency room. A boy is waiting for her. The boy fell off his bike. His wrist hurts, and he bumped his head.

The doctor examines the boy's injured head. It looks fine on the outside. But the doctor wants to make sure her patient does not have brain injuries. So, she

Sometimes doctors recommend holding ice packs on head injuries.

X-ray studies are a fast way to check for broken bones.

orders a computed tomography (CT) **scan**. The scan looks good. The boy has no broken bones in his skull. There is no bleeding inside his head either.

Then the doctor carefully touches the boy's wrist. She does not feel any broken bones. But the wrist is swollen. So, she orders an X-ray study. It does not show any problems either. She orders another test called a magnetic resonance imaging (MRI) scan. The boy lies still under a big MRI machine.

When the MRI scan is finished, the doctor has a better understanding of the boy's injury. Some **ligaments** are torn. The doctor bandages the wrist tightly. She puts the arm in a sling. She sends the boy home and tells him to rest. The wrist will start to heal on its own. Soon he will feel much better.

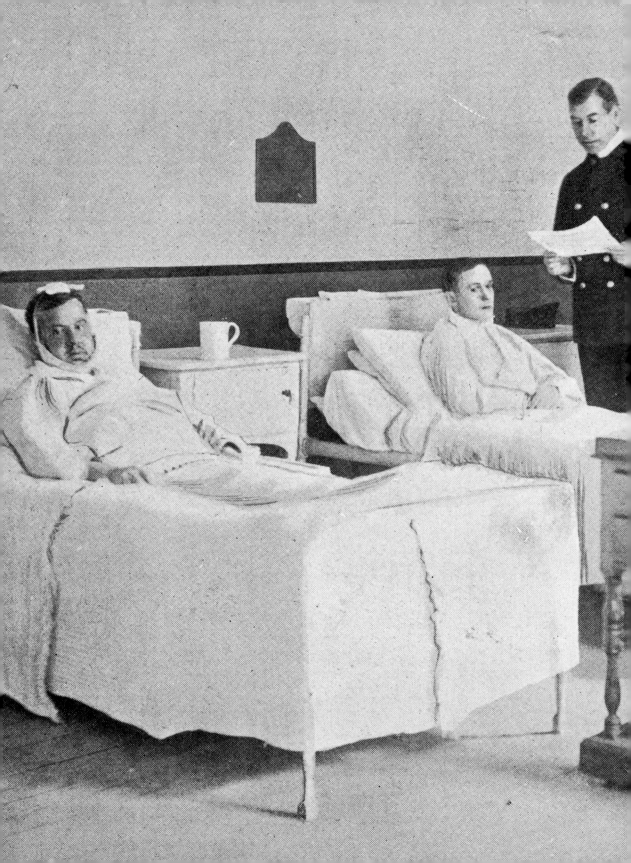

CHAPTER 2

EARLY WAYS TO DETECT INJURIES

In the past, it was hard for doctors to tell what was happening inside the body. They did not have machines that gave detailed pictures of bones, blood vessels, or other **tissues**.

For thousands of years, doctors **diagnosed** injuries by looking and feeling. They looked for cuts or bruises. They

Early hospitals and doctors' offices did not have very much technology.

After X-rays were invented, some doctors used them to find bullets in wounded soldiers.

watched for limping or felt for broken bones. These methods are useful. Doctors still use them today. But sometimes injuries can't be seen or felt from the outside.

In 1895, doctors gained a new tool to diagnose injuries. A German scientist discovered X-rays. These beams of energy are a type of **radiation**. An X-ray machine can send out X-rays. Hard body parts like bones block more of the X-rays. That makes bones look brighter on X-ray images. So, doctors began using X-rays to look for broken bones.

DISCOVERY OF X-RAYS

Wilhelm Röentgen discovered X-rays by accident. He was studying invisible energy beams that go through objects. He realized the beams could leave pictures on film. So, he used them to take a photo of his wife's hand. The photo showed bones underneath the skin. It also showed her wedding ring. The photo was printed in newspapers all over the world.

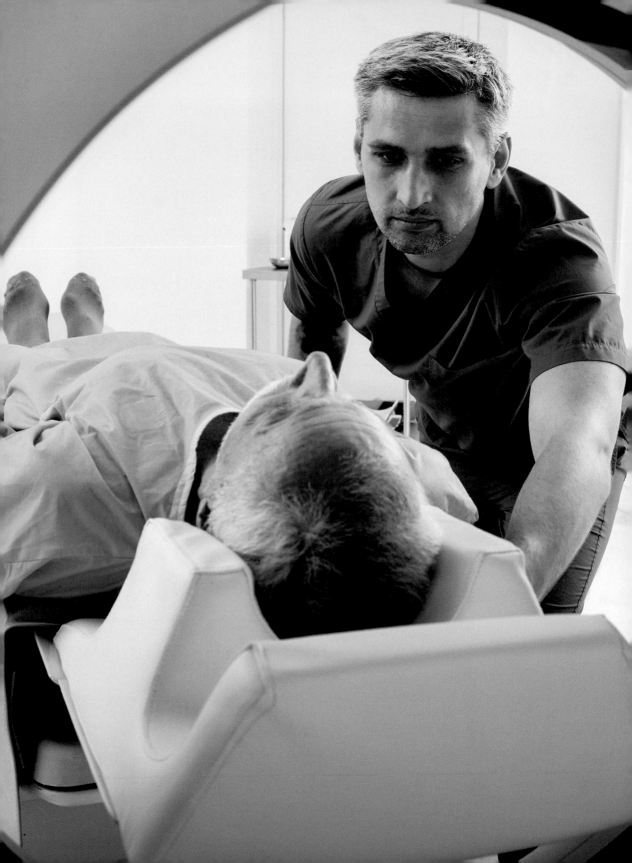

CHAPTER 3

DETECTING INJURIES TODAY

Today, doctors still use sight and touch to detect injuries. They still use X-rays, too. X-ray studies are great at showing bones. But they can't tell doctors much about the health of soft tissues. Newer methods can, though.

The first CT scan of a person took place in 1971. That let doctors see through the

New methods to detect injury often use complex machines. Health-care workers need special training to use the machines.

skull. For the first time, they could see the brain itself.

A CT scanner is shaped like a giant donut. The patient lies on a table that goes into the hole. X-ray beams go through the patient. Then, the machine makes pictures of the patient from different angles. The images are put together into stacks called slices. Doctors view the slices. They can see what the patient looks like on the inside. That helps them detect injuries.

CT scanners are very fast. Most scans take less than a minute. CT scanners also give detailed images. Some can even show the pictures in 3D.

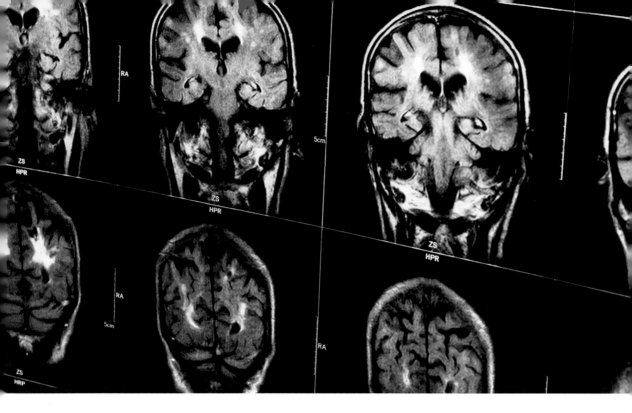

Slices of an MRI scan are like slices of a loaf of bread. Doctors can look at each slice to see inside the loaf.

In 1977, there was another important step forward. The first MRI scan was done. MRI scanners have powerful magnets. When a person goes in the middle of an MRI scanner, the person is surrounded by a powerful magnetic field. Then, hydrogen **protons** in the body

MRI scans do not have long-term side effects on patients.

move. They point toward the magnetic field. When radio waves are pulsed into the body, those protons shake. They send out new radio waves, and MRI scanners detect them. Different parts of the body have different amounts and types of the protons. MRI scanners process that information. Then the scanners use it to make images for doctors to review.

MRI and CT scans have enabled doctors to see inside the body more than they could before. These tools make it easier to detect injuries. That is a big help in treating patients.

IN THE AMBULANCE

Emergency medical technicians (EMTs) are often the first people to treat an injured patient. They arrive in an ambulance. But they don't have X-ray machines or CT scanners. So, they diagnose injuries by doing other tests and watching carefully. As the ambulance speeds toward the hospital, EMTs call doctors. They describe what they see. Doctors can be ready when the patient gets to the hospital.

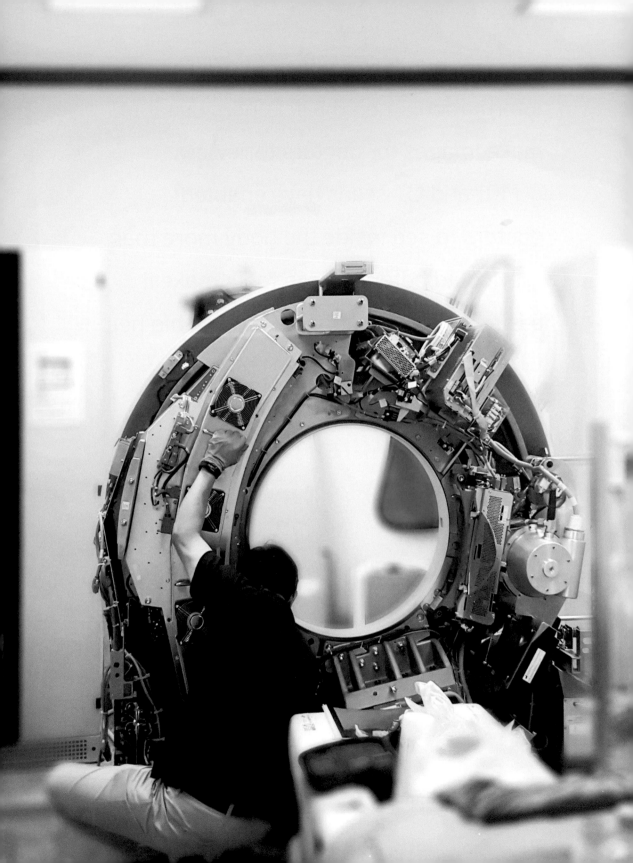

CHAPTER 4

PROBLEMS WITH CURRENT METHODS

X-ray studies, CT scans, and MRI scans are great at helping doctors detect injuries. But no tool is perfect.

CT scans use radiation to make pictures of patients' bodies. So do X-rays. Too much radiation can lead to health problems. Sometimes the risk of cancer could increase. Single CT scans or X-ray

Machines like CT scanners can break down. That can cause problems for doctors and patients.

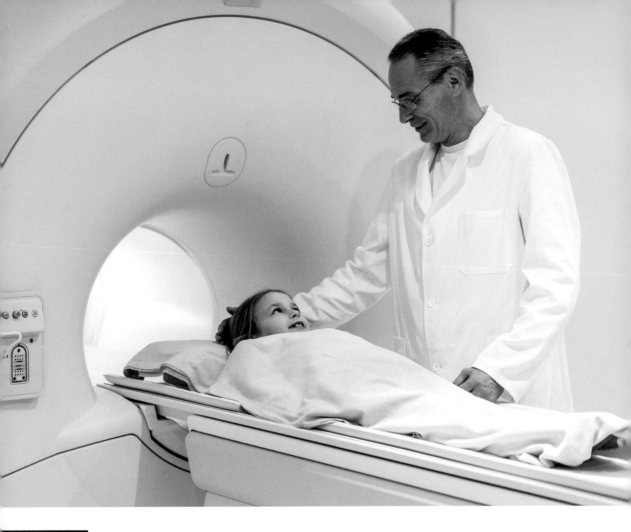

Babies, young children, and some people with special needs might have trouble staying still for MRI scans.

studies don't use much radiation. But if patients need a lot of scans, they might be exposed to high levels of radiation. That could harm their bodies.

MRI scans do not use radiation. They can still be dangerous, though. For example, MRI scanners have strong magnets. That means MRI scanning can't be used on patients with metal in their bodies. If the magnets pulled metal from their bodies into the machine, patients could be injured or even killed.

Most MRI scanners need patients to lie inside long tubes. It can be a tight fit. So, some patients may feel sick or scared. Another problem is movement. Patients have to lie still for a long time inside MRI scanners. If they don't, the images will be blurry. Staying still can be hard for some people, especially young children.

Doctors may give young patients **anesthesia** to help. But anesthesia has its own risks.

Although they have problems, CT scans and MRI scans are valuable tools. Doctors consider the risks and benefits to make good decisions for their patients.

DETECTING CONCUSSIONS

When people are hit in the head, they may get concussions. That is when the brain bounces back and forth and strikes the skull. Most concussions are not bad enough to show up on X-ray studies or scans. So, doctors diagnose concussions by observing **symptoms**. Common symptoms include headaches, dizziness, throwing up, or trouble walking and talking.

With these tools, the benefits are usually greater than the risks.

MRI SCAN VS. CT SCAN

MRI SCAN

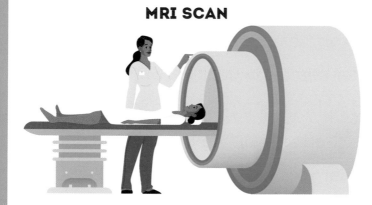

- very detailed
- no radiation
- slower
- more expensive

CT SCAN

- less detailed
- uses radiation
- faster
- cheaper

MAKE IT SMALL

X-ray studies, CT scans, and MRI scans are helpful for detecting injuries. But the machines that make these images are large. They cannot be moved easily.

For this reason, scientists are working on ways to make smaller detection devices. Small devices could be used right after a patient is injured. They could be used at sporting events or on battlefields. That way, patients would not have to wait to go to a hospital.

Some scientists created a small device called the Infrascanner. It scans a person's head. This tool uses light to look for problems such as blood clots. The device is small enough to fit in a person's hand.

Scientists have also made a moveable MRI scanner. It can be used outside of a hospital.

The Infrascanner can be used to check for bleeding inside the skull.

It even comes with its own power supply. It is not as good as large MRI scanners. But it can help patients who are far from hospitals.

CHAPTER 5

FUTURE DETECTION

Scientists are still looking for better ways to diagnose injuries. Some new machines look for proteins in a patient's blood. When the brain is hurt, proteins leak out of damaged cells. That might not show up on a CT scan. But new devices can detect the proteins and find injuries. The tests are also fast. They show results

Some brain injuries get better quickly. Others can be very serious.

Smart technology can make helmets and vision shields that help detect possible sickness as well as injury.

after just a few minutes. That could be very helpful for doctors.

Another new test looks for certain chemicals. These chemicals appear in the blood after head injuries. The test scans the patient's blood with a beam of light. Doctors can diagnose and treat the patient very quickly. That way, the patient can get better faster.

Companies are also working on **smart** clothing and equipment. These items can detect an injury as soon as it happens. The clothing has sensors that measure movements and forces. For example, a sensor inside a helmet can detect a strong hit that could injure a player. That means athletes could be treated right away. Smart clothing could even help athletes avoid injury in the first place. Doctors hope all these technologies will help improve patients' health.

FOCUS ON
DETECTING INJURY

Write your answers on a separate piece of paper.

1. Write a paragraph that compares two different ways to detect injury.

2. If you were injured, would you rather have a CT scan or an MRI scan? Why?

3. Which machine uses a magnet to detect injuries?

> **A.** CT scanner
> **B.** MRI scanner
> **C.** X-ray machine

4. What harm could happen if an injury is not detected for a long time?

> **A.** The injury could spread to other people.
> **B.** The injury could become worse over time.
> **C.** The injury could stay the same until it is detected.

Answer key on page 32.

GLOSSARY

anesthesia
Drugs that put people to sleep during medical procedures.

diagnosed
Identified an illness or disease.

ligaments
Bands of tough tissue that connect bones.

protons
Tiny bits of matter that have a positive electric charge.

radiation
Energy in the form of waves or particles.

scan
An image that shows the inside of the body.

smart
Containing computer technology that is programmed to analyze data.

symptoms
Signs of an illness or a disease.

tissues
Groups of cells in the body that have certain functions.

TO LEARN MORE

BOOKS

Hulick, Kathryn. *Medical Robots*. Minneapolis: Abdo Publishing, 2019.

Silverman, Buffy. *Cutting-Edge Medicine*. Minneapolis: Lerner Publications, 2020.

Thomas, Rachael L., and Josep Rural. *X-rays: A Graphic History*. Minneapolis: Graphic Universe, 2022.

NOTE TO EDUCATORS

Visit **www.focusreaders.com** to find lesson plans, activities, links, and other resources related to this title.

INDEX

Answer Key: 1. Answers will vary; **2.** Answers will vary; **3.** B; **4.** B